Quirky Wacky
Christmas Songs

A great collection of 17 easy-to-play songs

WISE PUBLICATIONS
part of The Music Sales Group
London/New York/Paris/Sydney/Copenhagen/Berlin/Madrid/Tokyo

Published by
Wise Publications
14-15 Berners Street,
London W1T 3LJ, UK.

Exclusive Distributors:
Music Sales Limited
Distribution Centre, Newmarket Road,
Bury St Edmunds, Suffolk IP33 3YB, UK.

Music Sales Pty Limited
20 Resolution Drive, Caringbah,
NSW 2229, Australia.

Order No. AM998646
ISBN 978-1-84938-268-7
This book © Copyright 2009 by Wise Publications,
a division of Music Sales Limited.

Arranging & Engraving supplied by Camden Music.
Music edited by Ann Farmer.
Compiled by Nick Crispin.

Printed in the EU.

Your Guarantee of Quality
As publishers, we strive to produce every book to the highest commercial standards.
The music has been carefully designed to minimise awkward page turns and to make playing from it a real pleasure.
Particular care has been given to specifying acid-free, neutral-sized paper made from pulps
which have not been elemental chlorine bleached. This pulp is from farmed sustainable forests
and was produced with special regard for the environment.
Throughout, the printing and binding have been planned to ensure
a sturdy, attractive publication which should give years of enjoyment.
If your copy fails to meet our high standards, please inform us and
we will gladly replace it.

www.musicsales.com

Grandma Got Run Over By A Reindeer

Words & Music by Stuart Brooks

Christmas Dinner

Words & Music by Tennessee Ernie Ford

9

Does Santa Claus Sleep With His Whiskers Over Or Under The Sheet?

Words & Music by Billy Bray & Fred Gibson

he go to bed with them tucked in his vest, and when he sleeps do they tick-le his chest?

I know a fat lad in Wig-an, whose bed-clothes won't co-ver his feet, but does

San-ta Claus sleep with his whisk-ers ov-er or un-der the sheet?

Grandfather Kringle

Words & Music by Stephen Gale & Leo Paris

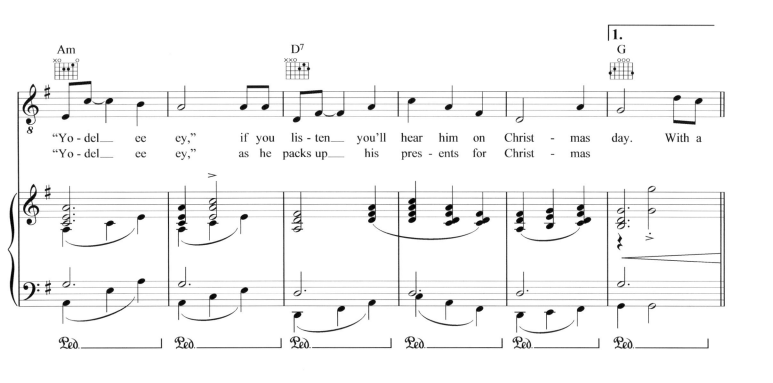

"Yo - del__ ee ey," if you lis - ten__ you'll hear him on Christ - mas day. With a
"Yo - del__ ee ey," as he packs up__ his pres - ents for Christ - mas

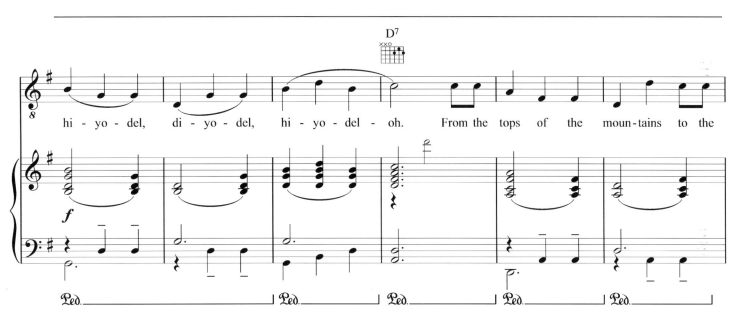

hi - yo - del, di - yo - del, hi - yo - del - oh. From the tops of the moun - tains to the

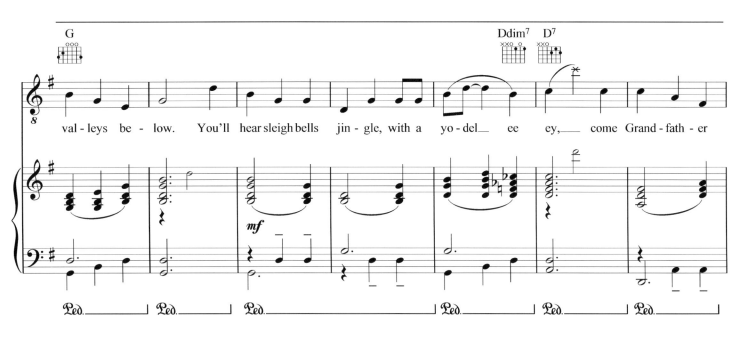

val - leys be - low. You'll hear sleigh bells jin - gle, with a yo - del__ ee ey,__ come Grand - fath - er

le - he, le - ee - hee!   There's a

gift in his bun - dle for each girl and boy,   for he knows just ex - act - ly what
wake in the mor - ning they look all a - round,   but__ Grand - fath - er Krin - gle is

toys they'll en - joy.   And it seems in their dreams they'll hear "Yo - del__ hee - ey,"   as he
not to be found.   But__ high in the moun - tains is "Yo - del__ hee - ey,"   from__

brings them their pres - ents on Christ - mas day.   With a hi - yo - del, di - yo - del,
Grand - fath - er Krin - gle on Christ - mas

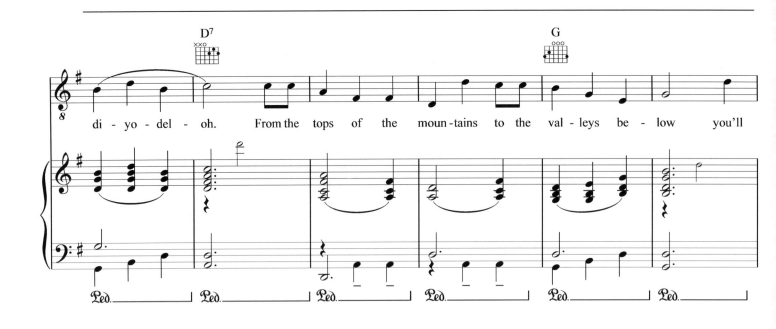

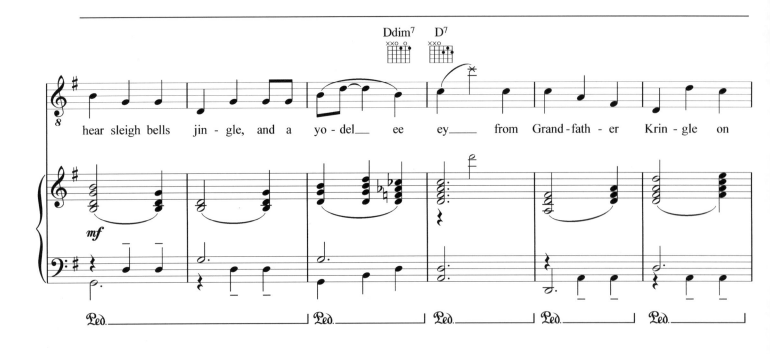

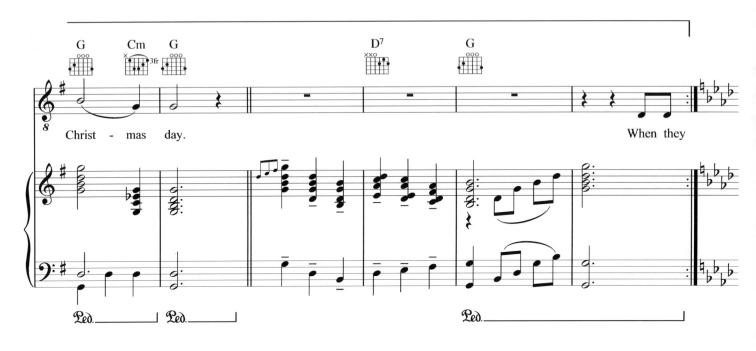

18

Here Comes Santa Claus

Words & Music by Gene Autry & Oakley Haldeman

Here comes San - ta Claus. Here comes San - ta Claus, right down San - ta Claus Lane.

Vix - en and Blitz - en and all his rein - deer are pull - in' on the reins.

He's got a bag that's_ filled with toys for the girls and boys a - gain.

I Want A Hippopotamus For Christmas

Words & Music by John Rox

The Little Fir Tree

Words & Music by Howard Barnes, Dominic John & Harold Corneilus

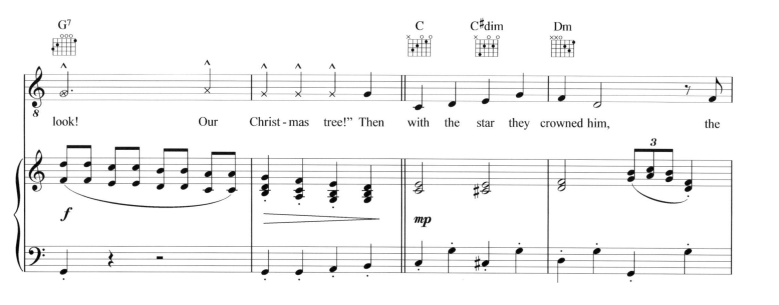

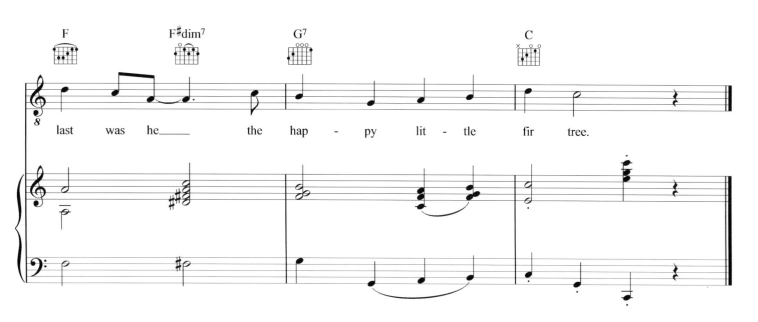

I'm A Little Christmas Cracker

Words & Music by Cosy Lee

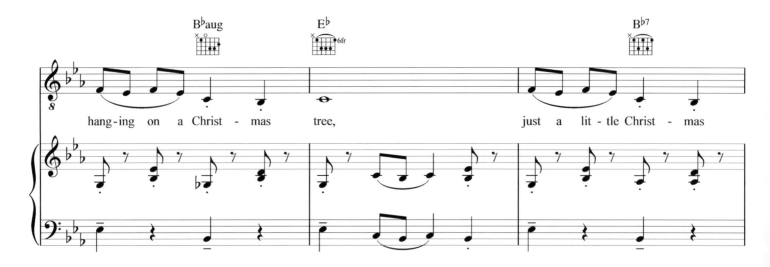

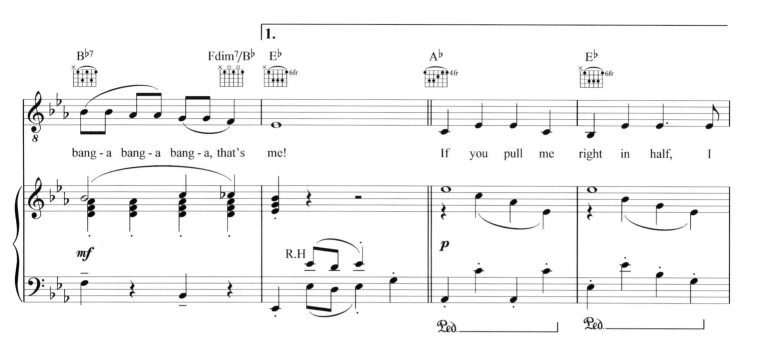

bang-a bang-a bang-a, that's me! If you pull me right in half, I

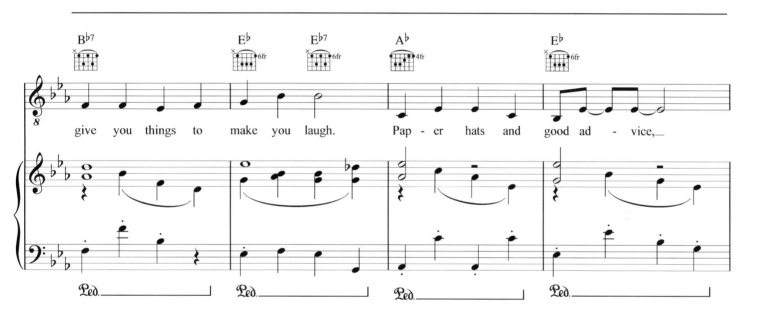

give you things to make you laugh. Pap-er hats and good ad - vice,___

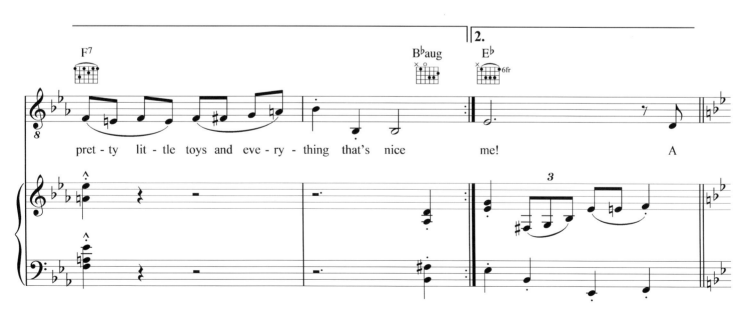

pret-ty lit-tle toys and eve-ry-thing that's nice me! A

Little Red Riding Hood's Christmas Tree

Words & Music by D. Donez, E. Dawson & A. Donne

Mele Kalikimaka
(Merry Christmas In Hawaii)

Words & Music by R. Alex Anderson

1.

Em⁷ ... A ... D ... A⁷

say 'mer-ry Christ-mas   to   you!'

2.

Em⁷ ... A⁷ ... Em⁷ ... A⁷

say 'mer-ry Christ-mas,   a   ve-ry mer-ry Christ-mas,   a

Em⁷ ... A⁷ ... D⁶ ... A⁷ ... D⁶ Ddim⁷ D

ve-ry, ve-ry, ve-ry mer-ry Christ-mas to   you!'

like a Hawaiian guitar

Little Snowman, Little Snowgirl

Words & Music by Johnny Sheridan, Ralph Ruvin, Bob Halfin & Harold Irvin

Mistletoe Kiss

Words & Music by James Kennedy & Constance Carpenter

"Blame it on the mi - stle-toe kiss!"

When the

Lots of fun you're

sure to miss if you don't get that mi - stle - toe kiss!

47

Never Do A Tango With An Eskimo

Words & Music by Tommie Connor

es - ki - mo!___ No! No! No! Oh dear no!___ If you

do you'll get the breeze up and you'll end up with a freeze up. You must ne - ver do a tan - go with an

es - ki - mo!___ No, no, no, no, no, no, no, no, no!

Santa's Little Sleigh Bells

Words & Music by Navarre & Cole

Suzy Snowflake

Words & Music by Sid Tepper & Roy Brodsky

55

The Wonderful Christmas Pig

Words & Music by Rolf Harris

Thirty-Two Feet And Eight Little Tails

Words & Music by James Cavanaugh, John Redmond & Frank Weldon